CHARLIE'S PARK

LION ON THE LOOSE!

WRITTEN BY
LOUISE NELSON

ILLUSTRATED BY
DRUE RINTOUL

BookLife freedom Readers

BookLife PUBLISHING

©2022 BookLife Publishing Ltd.
King's Lynn, Norfolk, PE30 4LS, UK

ISBN 978-1-80155-530-2

All rights reserved. Printed in Poland.

A catalogue record for this book is available from the British Library.

Charlie's Park: Lion on the Loose!
Written by Louise Nelson
Edited by Robin Twiddy
Illustrated & Designed by Drue Rintoul

Main title font courtesy of Josep.Ng via Shutterstock.com

ABOUT THE AUTHOR

Louise Nelson is an avid reader, writer and lover of stories. As a child, Louise would stay at home to write stories for her grandparents whilst her older brothers and sister played outside with the other local children. The exploits of her own children have been a constant source of inspiration in her writing, feeding little details of unmistakable authenticity into her child characters. Louise has written many books for BookLife Publishing and she hopes to author many more in the future.

ABOUT THE ILLUSTRATOR

Born and raised in King's Lynn, Norfolk, Drue has been a member of the BookLife team for over 7 years, where he has designed and illustrated more than 200 books. He has had a passion for illustration since he was a child, and continues to pursue this love both inside and outside of work. He resides in King's Lynn with his partner, Amy, and their cat, Sprout.

MEET THE CHARACTERS!

Uncle Monty

Charlie

Archie

Chapter 1
Just Another Day

In lots of ways, Charlie is just a regular kid. Each morning, he gets up, cleans his teeth and eats breakfast, just like you do. He puts on his school clothes, just like you do, and he packs his homework books into his backpack, just like you do.

But have you ever opened your school bag to find a

monkey inside? No?

Did you ever have to tell your teacher that a crocodile actually *did* eat your homework? No?

Have you ever been late for school because there was a giraffe in your garden? No?

Well, Charlie has!

This is because in other ways, Charlie's life is far from regular. Charlie doesn't live in a town or a city, like you. Charlie lives here, in Charlie's Park, the biggest nature reserve in the world!

CHARLIE'S PARK

Charlie's parents own the park. Charlie's mum is a famous explorer and his dad is a vet. Together, they built a park where all animals could live. Each zone of the park was made just the way the animals liked it. From lush rainforest to dry desert, they made a safe home for all animals in Charlie's Park.

Charlie and his brother,

Archie, live in the park. They go to school in the park and they look after the animals after school. There are lots of different animals living there and lots of things to learn. Charlie and Archie might not have a normal life, but they wouldn't have it any other way. Every day is exciting in Charlie's Park!

Chapter 2
Fence Failure!

It was Tuesday morning and Charlie and Archie had eaten breakfast, fed the tigers and caught a lift to school on a passing giraffe. It was a pretty typical day in the park.

At the front of the class stood Uncle Monty. Charlie liked Uncle Monty. Uncle Monty was the park's inventor. He made gadgets, gizmos and high-tech devices to help with life in the park. Some of them were even helpful. Uncle Monty was also the teacher. He taught science, common sense, good cookery and most importantly, all about the animals that lived in the park.

The best thing about having Uncle Monty as a teacher was that he was rather easily distracted.

Charlie only had to say, "Uncle Monty? What's that?" Then, Uncle Monty would forget all about the lesson. Instead, he would show you his latest invention.

Today, the children were supposed to be learning maths. What they were actually watching was Uncle

Monty spinning a glowing green rope above his head.

"You see, children," said Uncle Monty, "it's just like a regular lasso, but WITH LASERS!"

Uncle Monty threw the lasso towards a desk. The glowing green loop expanded until it was wider than the desk. It then tightened until it was firmly wrapped around the desk.

"The good thing about lasers," said Uncle Monty as he raised a large machete above his head, "is that they don't break!"

The machete bounced off the glowing green rope.

Archie let out a giggle as the large blade lodged itself in the ceiling.

Just then, a loud noise filled the classroom.

BEEP. BEEP. BEEP.

Uncle Monty and Charlie raced over to the big screen. It was filled with a map of the park. A bright red star was flashing on the screen.

"Oh no," said Uncle Monty. "What does a red star mean?"

"I know what it means," said Charlie. "Fence breach!"

Chapter 3
Lion on the Loose

The map allowed Monty to keep track of the whole park from his classroom.

"Fence breached in... sector three," said Uncle Monty.

"That's the Savannah Sector," Charlie replied.

"Uh-oh," said Archie. "Lion on the loose!"

Uncle Monty looked at the

map. Charlie's parents were far away, on the other side of the park. The Savannah Sector was just around the corner from the school.

"I bet this is Cedric, up to his old tricks again," Uncle Monty told the boys.

"Who's Cedric?" asked Archie.

"Cedric is a very annoying

lion. Possibly the most annoying of all," Uncle Monty answered.

"Don't be silly, Uncle Monty," said Charlie. "Lions are proud, not annoying. Lions are fierce and brave. You taught us that!"

"Not this one," his uncle replied. "This lion likes to play pranks."

All the other animals knew Cedric. Cedric liked to think he was very sneaky. He liked to *prove* just how sneaky he was by creeping up very close to other animals, then jumping out at them with a big **ROAR!**

They never saw him coming and it always caused a panic.

Cedric's little trick caused

the Great Giraffe Getaway,
the Frenzied Flamingo Fiasco,
and the mayhem of the Great
Monkey Mishap... and that was
all just last month!
What was he up to now?

Could he have escaped through the fence? Was he off to harass the hippos?

"Come on, Archie," said Charlie. "Let's go and check it out!"

"Wait!" Uncle Monty called. "Before you go, take these. They might come in handy." He handed Charlie a bag full of interesting-looking gadgets. Was that a green glow coming from inside?

"You never know what you might need!"

Chapter 4
Where Did Cedric Go?

The brothers zoomed to the point in the fence that had triggered the alarm. Charlie drove Uncle Monty's quadbike. Archie clung on to his brothers back. Charlie noted how strong Archie's grip was. Their parents were right, Archie did have more in common with the monkeys than his actual family.

The fence itself wasn't damaged. Underneath, it was a different matter. There was a giant hole in the ground where someone – or something – had dug under the fence. Archie unzipped the bag and pulled out a tablet computer.

Charlie jumped down into the hole for a closer look.

While Archie used the camera on his tablet to scan the area, Charlie pushed his hands through the soil, looking for clues. It didn't take him long to find one. Snagged on the bottom of the fence was a collar. The collar had a name tag on it.

Charlie clicked in the button on his walkie talkie.

"It's just as you suspected, Uncle Monty. It's Cedric," Charlie said.

The device crackled in his hand. "Are you sure?"

"Yes. I've found his collar at the fence," Charlie told him.

"Charlie, quick. Come here. I've found some tracks,"

Archie said.

Charlie jumped up out of the hole and followed his brother, who was using his gadget to scan some footprints in the ground. "My computer reading says that a single lion went off in that direction."

"But that doesn't make sense," Charlie said.

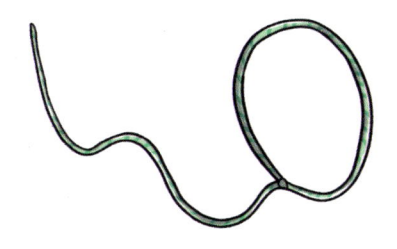

"Why not?" Archie asked. "Because that's the way to the Frozen Zone," Charlie told his brother. "Lions don't belong in the Frozen Zone."

Getting back on the quadbike, the brothers started following the tracks to the coldest section of the park. Both knew that things were about to get very chilly indeed.

Chapter 5
Lions Don't Like Snow

Cedric the lion must have thought that sneaking around the Frozen Zone would be rather fun. Unfortunately, it turned out that this place was called the Frozen Zone for a reason. Cedric was very cold. He had been walking through deep snow for a good ten minutes.

He hadn't even seen anything to sneak up on! Just one little penguin, and that had jumped into the water and swum off as soon as it had seen Cedric.

    Shivering because of the cold, Cedric was beginning to wish that he had stayed at home in the warmth of the Savannah Sector. Cedric started to think maybe he should just head home.

But wait! What was this?

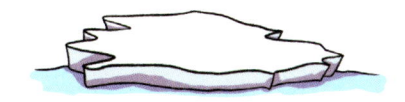

A cunning grin spread across Cedric's face. The cheeky old lion was walking along the edge of a giant ice sheet when he spotted it. Just below him was a little seal. It was floating along on an ice floe without a care in the world. The seal was asleep on the ice. He must have been enjoying the Sun after a morning spent fishing in the icy water. Cedric watched as the seal floated along to where

he was waiting.

Like all good lions, Cedric loved nothing better than to pounce on his victims. This poor little seal was no different. The lion crouched down... then sprang forward, down onto the ice floe below.

ROOAAR!

The big cat landed on one half of the floe. It sank down

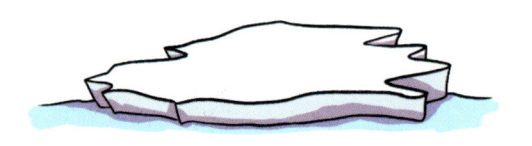

and the other side shot up, just like a seesaw, flinging the seal into the air. The poor thing woke up with a start as it loop-de-looped through the air. Like an acrobat, the seal righted itself and pointed its nose towards the water.

SPLOSH!

Dazed and confused, the little seal honked at Cedric and

swam off.

Cedric sniggered to himself because of his brilliant prank. That seal sure didn't expect a lion. Cedric looked around for a way back to solid ground.

There was only one problem. After his brilliant joke, the ice floe had drifted away from the shore. Cedric was stuck. He had a decision to make. He could float until he got to the other side of the lake, or he could get his paws wet and paddle back to shore.

Cedric was wet and cold. He wasn't a good swimmer. He didn't think either option sounded good. What would he do?

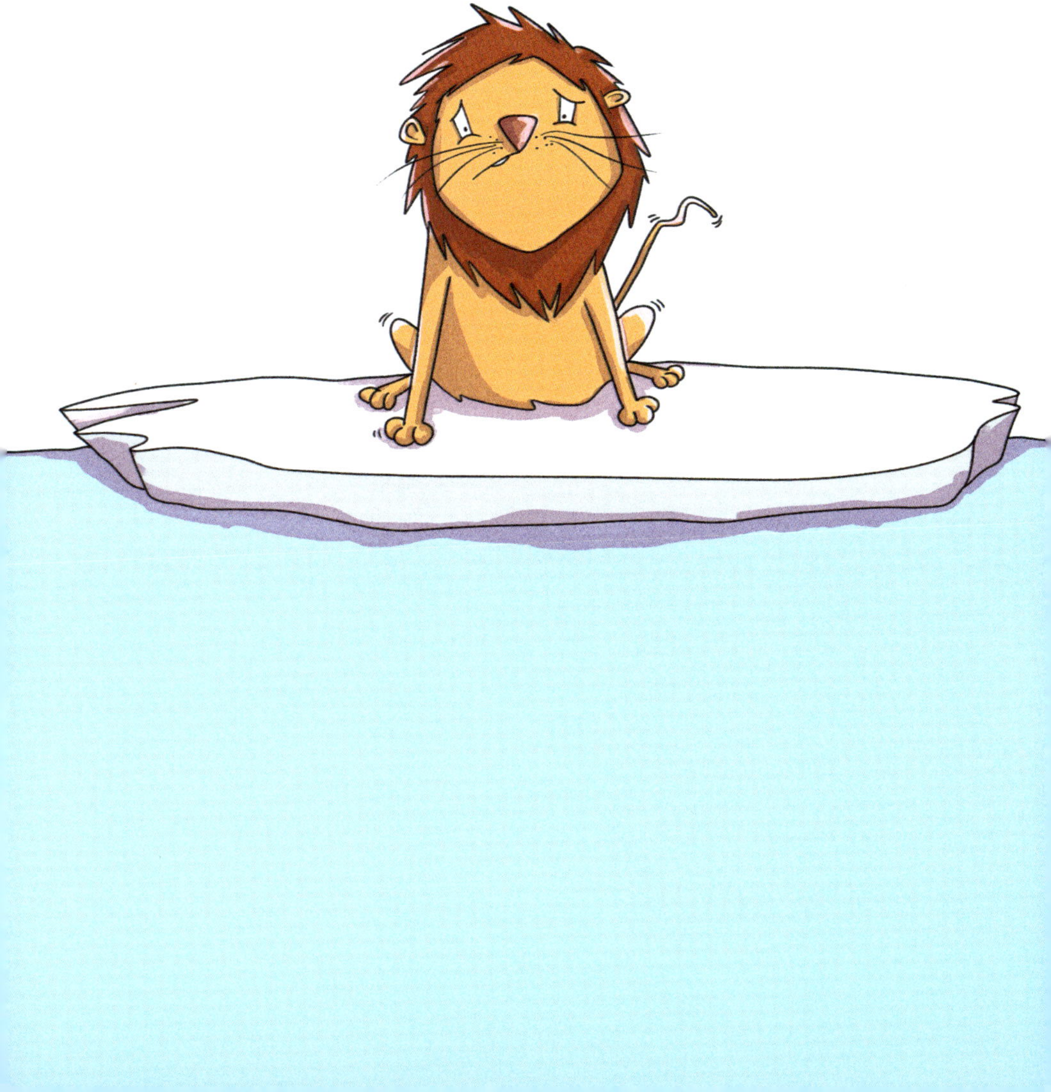

Chapter 6
Uh-oh – Orcas!

Cedric was about to start paddling when he saw something up ahead.
Oh no.

Just a few meters away, Cedric saw tall black fins sticking out of the water. They were all headed in his direction. Cedric backed away from the edge of his little lump of ice and watched nervously.

The first orca poked its head out of the water. It was quickly followed by the rest of its pod. The black-and-white orcas surrounded the ice floe. Cedric realised that he was in trouble. Perhaps all the tricks he'd been pulling on the other animals were about to bite him back.

The orcas looked at each other. They hadn't met Cedric before, but they'd heard about him. For starters, a young seal had just warned them that the lion was out causing trouble in the Frozen Zone. The orcas knew they were in charge around here. Sneaky lions didn't belong in their zone. Cedric needed to be taught a lesson.

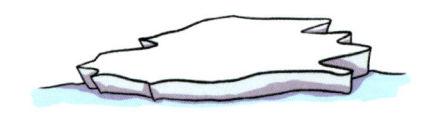

   The orcas decided to start having a little fun with the lion. Maybe they would see how he liked being scared for a change. The first orca nudged the floe with his nose, sending the lion scrambling.

The second one did the same. He nudged the ice back towards his friend. The third orca decided that she wanted a go too. She pushed the lion in yet another direction. Before long, the pod of orcas was batting the floe left and right,

right and left. Poor old Cedric was clinging on for dear life. His giant claws dug firmly into the ice.

If this was a prank, Cedric did not think it was funny!

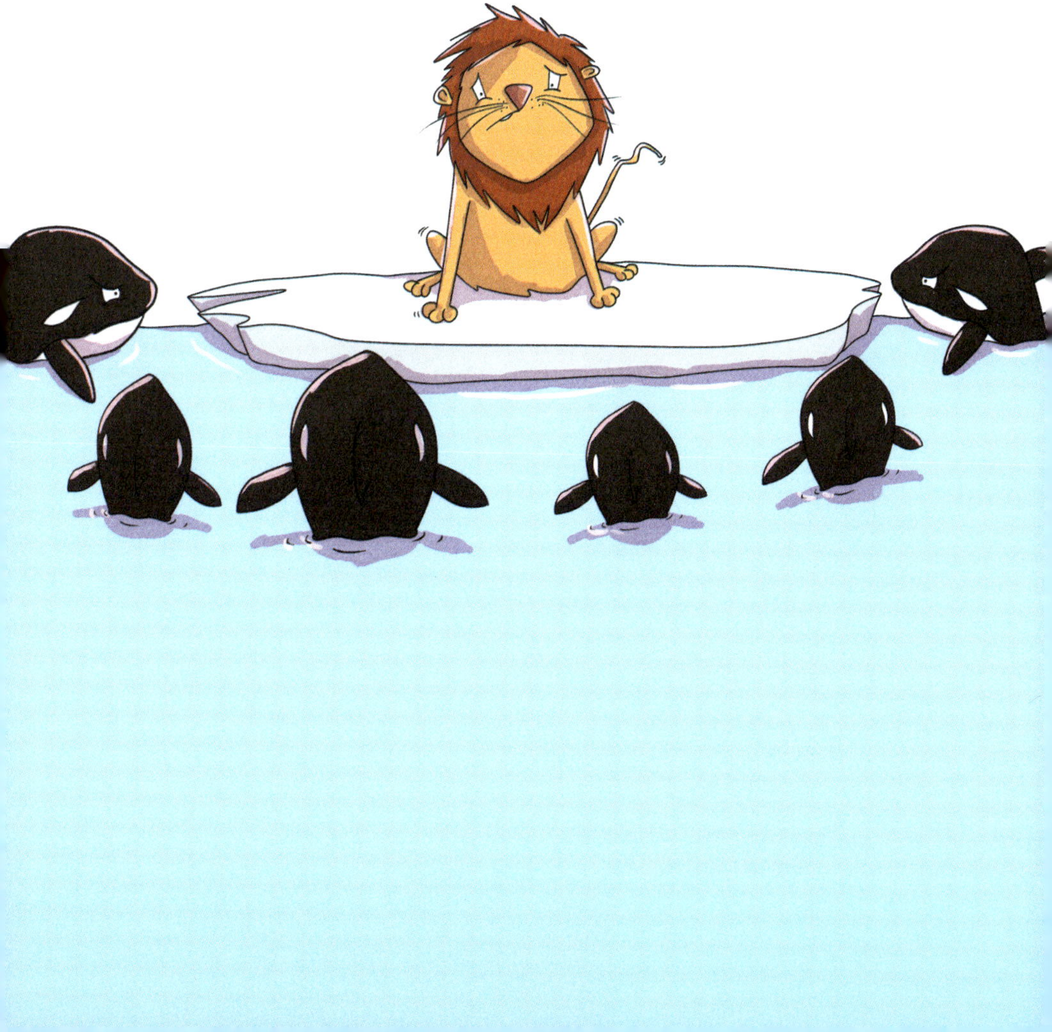

Chapter 7
The Laser Lasso!

Charlie and Archie skidded to a halt at the edge of the ice just in time to see Cedric growling at the orcas. "They're playing a prank on him," laughed Archie. "They're giving him a taste of his own medicine!"

"Lions don't belong in the icy sea," said Charlie. "We'd better get Cedric back to shore."

Luckily, Archie was already one step ahead. He pulled out Uncle Monty's bag of gadgets.

Inside was a selection of

weird and wonderful devices. The one that Archie was looking for was glowing green at the bottom of the bag – the laser lasso! Picking it up, Archie uncoiled the rope and got ready to throw it. It was very light and very bright.

    Archie twirled the green rope around in the air. The loop of the lasso whirled above him, shining green light across the snow. It was as light as a feather. Archie threw the rope towards Cedric. It flew through the air. The strange green light made the orcas look up for a second. The lasso hooked the ice floe.

"Great job, Archie!" said Charlie.

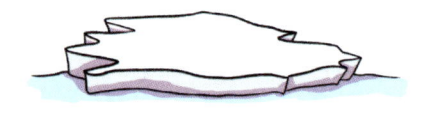

Archie started to pull in the lion. Cedric was very wet, very cold and very miserable. The orcas saw the lion being pulled to safety. They did not want their fun to end.

The pod started pushing Cedric away from the bank. Archie was pulled off the shore and into the water! He didn't let go. Instead, he pulled

himself onto the ice floe.
He sat next to the frozen lion,
both now very wet, very cold
and very miserable.

"Throw the lasso to me!"
Charlie yelled to Archie.

Archie sent the end
of the rope back onto the
shore. Charlie caught it.

Not wanting to get pulled in himself, Charlie tied the end of the rope onto the back of the quadbike. He started the engine.

This time, Charlie was able to use the power of the quadbike to pull the ice floe to shore. The wheels spun in the snow. Charlie hit a button on the handles, making thrusters at the back of the quad bike roar into life.

"Good old Uncle Monty," Charlie said to himself as the quad bike lurched forward, pulling the large ice floe towards the frozen land. As soon as they were close enough, Archie hopped onto the shore, dragging Cedric with him.

Chapter 8
A Lesson for a Lion

It was a tight squeeze, but they eventually managed to get the frozen lion onto the back of the quadbike. He had not been at all happy at first. Lions don't belong on quadbikes. But this frozen lion knew he didn't belong in the Frozen Zone either. He wanted to go home.

When they got there,

a very sheepish Cedric was happy to be home in the lion enclosure. Cedric was tired, cold and hungry. He hadn't had a bite to eat all day. After the accident in the Frozen Zone, he was very happy to see that it was almost feeding time for the big cats... even if the other lions were laughing at him a little bit.

As Cedric sat down to eat his dinner, he looked up at the giant glass screen. Three figures stood on the other side of it. He had been a little embarrassed to have been saved by a couple of small boys. At the same time, he was glad they had turned up when they did.

"I wonder what he's thinking about?" Archie said, turning to Charlie and Uncle Monty.

"I dare say he's thinking that he'll never sneak up on anyone again," Uncle Monty said with a wicked smile.

"I think he's just glad to be home," Charlie said. "He looks happy to be back."

And he was. Cedric chewed on his dinner. He was most pleased to be back at the lion enclosure.

He was also thinking about who he should *sneak* up on

tomorrow. He hadn't paid the hippos a visit in some time...

WARM WATERS

DESERT DOMES

MIGHTY MOUNTAINS

FROZEN OCEAN

RAINFOREST REGION

SAVANNAH SECTOR

TUNDRA TOWN

FROZEN ZONE